BRIGHT
IDEA
BOOKS

YOU CAN
WORK IN
Music

by Carolina Walker

raintree
a Capstone company — publishers for children

Raintree is an imprint of Capstone Global Library Limited, a company incorporated in England and Wales having its registered office at 264 Banbury Road, Oxford, OX2 7DY – Registered company number: 6695582

www.raintree.co.uk
myorders@raintree.co.uk

Edited by Charly Haley
Designed by Becky Daum
Production by Claire Vanden Branden
Originated by Capstone Global Library Ltd
Printed and bound in India

ISBN 978 1 4747 7530 4 (hardback)   ISBN 978 1 4747 7354 6 (paperback)
22 21 20 19 18   22 21 20 19 18
10 9 8 7 6 5 4 3 2 1   10 9 8 7 6 5 4 3 2 1

British Library Cataloguing in Publication Data
A full catalogue record for this book is available from the British Library.

Acknowledgements
We would like to thank the following for permission to reproduce photographs: iStockphoto: electravk, 10, FGorgun, cover (background), Monkeybusinessimages, 25, Pekic, 17, RoBeDeRo, 12–13, South_agency, 26–27, Xijian, 8–9; Shutterstock Images: 5 second Studio, 31, Brian A Jackson, 20–21, Nejron Photo , cover (foreground), 18–19, Nomad_Soul, 22–23, Prostock-studio, 5, Sirtravelalot, 15, Vectorfusionart, 6–7. Design Elements: iStockphoto, Red Line Editorial, and Shutterstock Images.

CONTENTS

CHAPTER 1

IN THE
Spotlight

Most people enjoy listening to music. But some make music every day. It's their job. They might love the energy of a concert. They might like writing songs. They work hard to make great music.

There are many jobs in music. Each one uses different **talents**. All jobs can be hard work. But they can be fun too.

Do you like listening to music? You might like to work in music when you grow up!

A singer may perform rock, pop, country or another type of music.

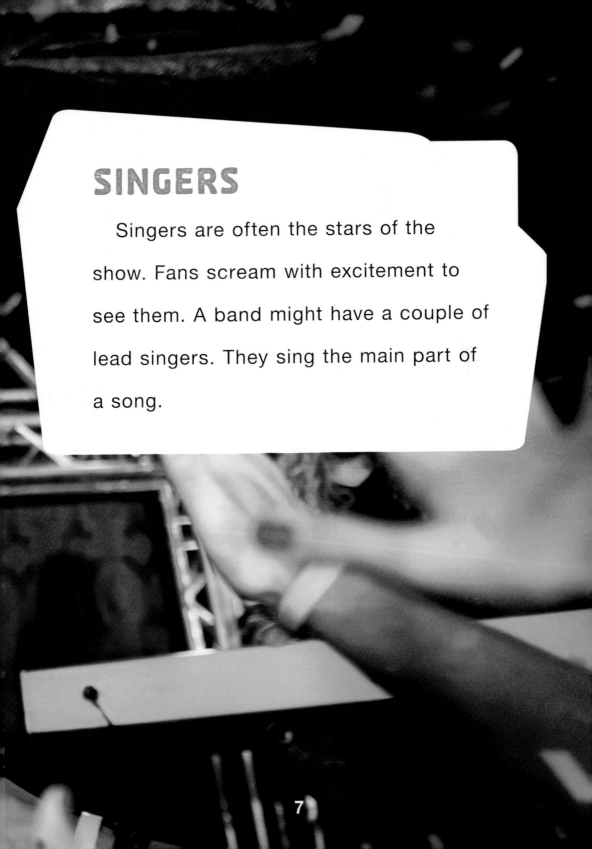

SINGERS

Singers are often the stars of the show. Fans scream with excitement to see them. A band might have a couple of lead singers. They sing the main part of a song.

Background singers help lead singers. They make songs sound stronger at concerts. They help on **recordings** of songs. They **harmonize** by singing notes that sound good with the lead singer's notes.

People in a band share fame. But some singers are alone in the spotlight. They are **solo** artists. Other people sing and act in musical plays. Their voices tell stories.

In a recording studio, a singer can record a song again and again. She works to make it sound perfect.

A singer must feel comfortable onstage.

Singers need **skill**. They need talent. But voice lessons are also important. Lessons teach singers how to use their voices well. Singers practise a lot. Their working hours are unusual. Concerts can go on late into the night.

LUCKY STARS

Only a few singers become famous. It takes talent and a lot of luck!

A musician may play outdoors or in a concert hall.

MUSICIANS

Musicians play instruments. Some play in bands. Others play solo. They might play at concerts. Or they might play on an album.

There are different types of music. Rock bands play loud concerts. Pop music sounds **catchy**. Some musicians **perform** classical music. This might be with a full orchestra. Orchestras have many instruments. They have violins, flutes, trumpets and more. Musicians need to play with skill.

Most musicians had music lessons when they were young. They learnt how music works. Music lessons teach all the ways to use an instrument. It takes a lot of practice to perform well.

Do you have a good ear for music? Do you love to practise? You might make a good singer or musician!

A musician must
practise a lot.

15

CHAPTER 2

BEHIND
the Scenes

There are many music jobs for people who don't want to perform. These jobs are behind the scenes. Some people write songs. Others make recordings sound good.

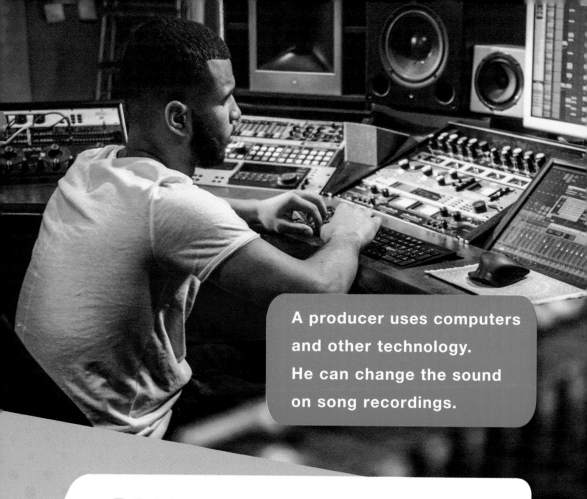

A producer uses computers and other technology. He can change the sound on song recordings.

SONGWRITERS

Some people write songs for bands. Some write songs for adverts. Others write music for a whole orchestra. Songwriters need creativity. They know what listeners will enjoy.

PRODUCERS

Producers help other people make music. They help make recordings sound good. Producers hire musicians for recordings. They handle the **budget** on music projects. A budget is a plan for how money is spent. Producers are usually skilled musicians. They need to have good attention to detail. They also need to be good with technology.

JINGLES

A songwriter can earn a living by writing songs for adverts. These songs are called jingles.

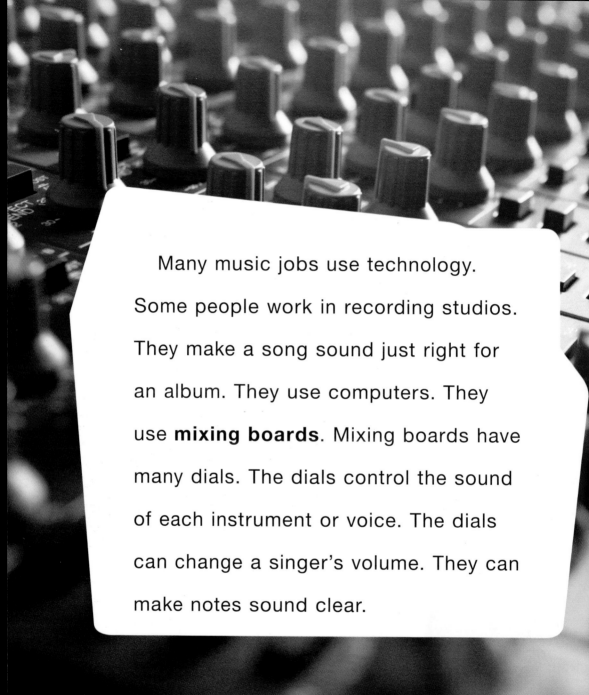

Many music jobs use technology.
Some people work in recording studios.
They make a song sound just right for
an album. They use computers. They
use **mixing boards**. Mixing boards have
many dials. The dials control the sound
of each instrument or voice. The dials
can change a singer's volume. They can
make notes sound clear.

A mixing board is used in a recording studio to make songs sound better.

CONCERTS

Some people control sound at concerts. They make live music loud and clear. All concerts need sound experts. These people set up speakers. They connect cables. They check the sound before a concert. They use mixing boards. They fix problems. Music should sound as good as possible for the audience.

A sound expert needs to be good with music and technology.

Most sound experts went to university. Teachers train students to use technology and sound equipment.

Are you good with technology? You might like working with sound. You might like working in a recording studio.

CHAPTER 3

TEACHING
Music

Music teachers give lessons to future singers or musicians. Music teachers can work in schools. Others teach from home. Many music teachers have been to university. They have learnt all about singing or how to play an instrument.

Are you good at music? Do you enjoy helping others learn? You might like teaching music.

A music teacher may offer piano lessons.

Having a job in music can be hard work. But people do it because they love music.

There are many exciting jobs in music. Some jobs use musical talent. Others use technology skills. Which job is right for your talents?

GOING PLACES

Many people travel for their music jobs. They even go to other countries!

GLOSSARY

budget
amount of money available for a project

catchy
easy to remember as a song or phrase

harmonize
when people sing different notes that sound good together

mixing board
board with dials that allows someone to adjust individual sounds in a recording or performance

perform
put on a show for an audience

recording
music that is stored on a computer or other location

skill
being able to do something well

solo
performing alone without another voice or instrument

talent
something a person is naturally good at

FIND OUT MORE

Want to learn more about making music? Check out these resources:

Books

Create Your Own Music (Media Genius), Matthew Anniss (Raintree, 2016)
Music (Behind the Scenes), Judith Henegan (Wayland, 2013)
Musical Instruments (How Things Work), Ade Dean-Pratt (Wayland, 2013)
Start a Band! (Find Your Talent), Matt Anniss (Franklin Watts, 2014)

Website

www.dkfindout.com/uk/music-art-and-literature/types-music
Find out more about different types of music.

Places to visit

British Music Experience, Liverpool
www.britishmusicexperience.com
Learn about the music scene in the UK!

Royal Academy of Music Museum, London
www.ram.ac.uk/museum
This museum has a large collection of musical instruments, paintings and letters to see.

ACTIVITY

WRITE WORDS FOR A SONG

1. Pick your favourite song. With an adult's help, find the words to the song online.

2. Think about what the song's words mean. Pick a different story to tell with your song. For example, your new song could be about a funny moment in your life, a fun activity you did with friends or a special place you like to visit.

3. Look at the original song's words. Make a slash at every syllable in a word. Count the syllables in each line. Circle the words that rhyme.

For example, listen to this old song, "The Ballad of Casey Jones", on your computer. Look at the words.

1   2   3   4   5   6   7   8   9   (10)

Come/ all/ you/ round/ers/, if/ you/ wan/'to/ hear

1 2   3 4   5   6   7   (8 9 10)

A/ sto/ry/ a/bout/ a/ brave/ en/gi/neer/

4. Now write new words for the song so it is about the topic you chose. Try to keep the same number of syllables in each line and rhyme in the same places.

Example:

Sit in my tree house if you want to see

The birds soaring high and singing to me

5. Now perform your song! Sing your song to the same tune as the original song. You could sing it for family or friends.

INDEX